Crypto Revolution: Transformi World Economy

In this groundbreaking book, Crypto Revolution: Transforming the World Economy, we explore the rapid emergence and transformative power of cryptocurrency in today's world. The economy was once flourishing under traditional financial systems, but the recent boom of crypto has revolutionized the way we perceive and engage with money. This book delves into the reasons behind this extraordinary shift and examines how cryptocurrencies will continue to enhance the global economic landscape.

As technology advances, the intersection of artificial intelligence and cryptocurrencies becomes increasingly significant. AI research has the potential to revolutionize the world of crypto, offering new insights, improving security, and enabling more efficient transactions. This book investigates the profound impact of AI on the future of cryptocurrencies and how it will reshape the world's economic fiat system.

With expert analysis and thought-provoking discussions, Crypto Revolution takes you on a journey through the history, mechanics, and implications of cryptocurrencies. It examines how blockchain technology, the backbone of cryptocurrencies, is transforming industries and empowering individuals. By decentralizing financial systems, cryptocurrencies offer unparalleled opportunities for innovation, financial inclusion, and economic growth.

Join us as we explore the challenges and opportunities presented by the crypto space. From regulatory frameworks and investment strategies to the environmental impact of crypto mining, this book provides a comprehensive understanding of the crypto landscape. Additionally, it sheds light on the growing trend of central bank digital currencies, potentially revolutionizing the concept of money as we know it.

Prepare to embark on an eye-opening exploration of the socioeconomic implications of the crypto revolution. Discover how cryptocurrencies are reshaping economies, challenging traditional financial institutions, and empowering individuals worldwide. Get ready for a glimpse into the future of finance and the transformative power of crypto.

Contents

Chapter 1: The Rise of Cryptocurrency

Cryptocurrency, once an obscure concept limited to tech enthusiasts, has emerged as a disruptive force reshaping the world of finance and economics. In this chapter, we will explore the origins of cryptocurrency, the factors that contributed to its rise, and the implications of its growing popularity.

1.1 The Genesis of Cryptocurrency

The story of cryptocurrency begins with the enigmatic figure known as Satoshi Nakamoto. In 2008, Nakamoto published a whitepaper titled "Bitcoin: A Peer-to-Peer Electronic Cash System," introducing the world to the first decentralized digital currency. Bitcoin, the pioneer of cryptocurrencies, laid the foundation for a new era of financial innovation.

1.2 Digital Currency vs. Traditional Currency

To understand the rise of cryptocurrency, we must first examine the limitations of traditional currency. Fiat money, backed by governments and central banks, is subject to inflation, manipulation, and cumbersome cross-border transactions. Cryptocurrencies offer an alternative that addresses these issues by leveraging blockchain technology.

1.3 Trust in Decentralization

One of the fundamental aspects that propelled the rise of cryptocurrency is the concept of decentralization. Traditional financial systems rely on intermediaries such as banks to facilitate transactions and maintain trust. Cryptocurrencies, on the other hand, utilize decentralized networks where transactions are verified by a distributed ledger called the blockchain. This eliminates the need for intermediaries and puts control back in the hands of individuals.

1.4 Security and Transparency

Cryptocurrencies provide enhanced security and transparency compared to traditional financial systems. The cryptographic algorithms used in cryptocurrencies ensure secure transactions and protect against fraud and hacking attempts. Furthermore, the blockchain's transparent nature allows anyone to view transaction histories, promoting accountability and reducing the risk of corruption.

1.5 Financial Inclusion and Empowerment

One of the most significant advantages of cryptocurrency is its potential for financial inclusion. In many parts of the world, traditional banking services are inaccessible to large segments of the population. Cryptocurrencies provide an opportunity for individuals without access to banking infrastructure to participate in the global economy, opening doors to economic empowerment and financial independence.

1.6 Early Adopters and Market Growth

In the early years of cryptocurrency, a small community of enthusiasts experimented with Bitcoin and other digital currencies. Over time, as more individuals recognized the benefits and potential of cryptocurrencies, the market experienced exponential growth. The rise of cryptocurrency exchanges and the proliferation of alternative coins (altcoins) expanded the ecosystem, attracting investors, entrepreneurs, and developers from various industries.

1.7 Challenges and Regulatory Landscape

While the rise of cryptocurrency brought remarkable opportunities, it also presented challenges. Governments and regulators struggled to keep pace with this rapidly evolving field. Concerns about money laundering, tax evasion, and consumer protection prompted the implementation of regulations to ensure the responsible use of cryptocurrencies. Balancing innovation and security remains an ongoing task for policymakers worldwide.

1.8 Cryptocurrency's Impact on Industries

As cryptocurrencies gained prominence, their impact extended beyond finance. Industries such as supply chain management, healthcare, and voting systems have started exploring the potential applications of blockchain technology. Smart contracts, powered by cryptocurrencies, emerged as a means to automate and streamline business processes, enhancing efficiency and reducing costs.

1.9 The Future of Cryptocurrency

The rise of cryptocurrency is just the beginning of a transformative journey. As technology advances and adoption increases, cryptocurrencies are poised to revolutionize not only the financial industry but also sectors like real estate, art, and gaming. The integration of cryptocurrencies with emerging technologies such as artificial intelligence and the Internet of Things will further amplify their potential.

In this chapter, we have witnessed the remarkable rise of cryptocurrency, from its humble beginnings to its current status as a global phenomenon. The next chapters will delve deeper into the mechanisms of blockchain technology, the impact of cryptocurrencies on financial markets, and how they are transforming the global economy. Join us on this exciting journey as we explore the world of cryptography and its profound implications.

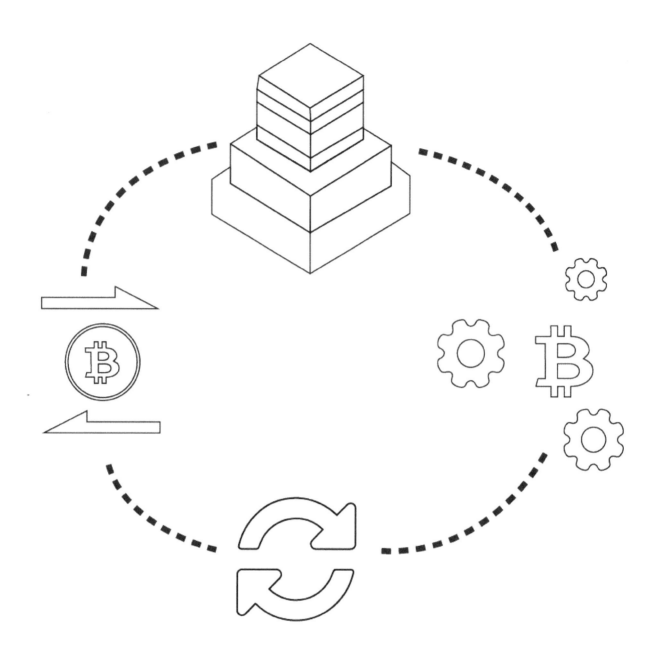

Chapter 2: The Evolution of Traditional Economics

The world of economics has witnessed a remarkable evolution throughout history. In this chapter, we will explore the foundations of traditional economics, its key theories and models, and the factors that led to its evolution in response to changing economic landscapes.

2.1 The Birth of Traditional Economics

Traditional economics, also known as classical economics, traces its roots back to the 18th century and the works of influential thinkers such as Adam Smith and David Ricardo. Their theories emphasized the principles of supply and demand, market competition, and the efficiency of free markets as drivers of economic growth and prosperity.

2.2 The Neoclassical Revolution

The late 19th century marked the rise of neoclassical economics, which built upon classical theories while introducing new concepts and mathematical modeling. Neoclassical economists sought to understand consumer behavior, the allocation of resources, and the equilibrium of markets through concepts like marginal utility, rational choice theory, and general equilibrium analysis.

2.3 Keynesian Economics and Macroeconomics

The Great Depression of the 1930s challenged the tenets of neoclassical economics and paved the way for the emergence of Keynesian economics. John Maynard Keynes argued for the importance of government intervention to mitigate economic downturns and promote full employment. This gave rise to the field of macroeconomics, which focuses on the study of aggregate economic phenomena such as inflation, unemployment, and economic growth.

2.4 Monetarism and the Quantity Theory of Money

In the mid-20th century, monetarism gained prominence as an alternative to Keynesian economics. The monetarists, led by Milton Friedman, emphasized the role of the money supply and its impact on inflation and economic stability. The quantity theory of money, which posits a direct relationship between the money supply and price levels, became a fundamental principle of monetarist thought.

2.5 The Emergence of Behavioral Economics

Traditional economics assumed that individuals always acted rationally and in their own self-interest. However, the field of behavioral economics, pioneered by scholars like Daniel Kahneman and Richard Thaler, challenged this assumption. Behavioral economists studied how psychological biases and cognitive limitations influence economic decision-making, highlighting the importance of understanding human behavior in economic analysis.

2.6 The Rise of New Economic Paradigms

In recent decades, new economic paradigms have emerged, driven by advancements in technology, globalization, and the recognition of social and environmental factors. Institutional economics focuses on the role of institutions and their impact on economic systems, while ecological economics integrates environmental considerations into economic analysis. Additionally, feminist economics examines the role of gender in economic systems and strives for gender equity.

2.7 Challenges and Critiques of Traditional Economics

Traditional economics has faced criticism for its assumptions of perfect competition, rational behavior, and a limited focus on monetary factors. Critics argue that it fails to account for real-world complexities such as income inequality, market failures, and externalities. Alternative economic frameworks have emerged to address these shortcomings and provide a more comprehensive understanding of economic phenomena.

2.8 The Interdisciplinary Approach and Modern Economics

The evolution of traditional economics has increasingly embraced interdisciplinary approaches. Economists now collaborate with experts from fields such as psychology, sociology, computer science, and data analytics to gain deeper insights into economic behavior, complex systems, and the impact of emerging technologies. This multidisciplinary approach enriches economic analysis and enables a more nuanced understanding of the global economy.

2.9 The Future of Economics

As the world continues to change at a rapid pace, economics will undoubtedly evolve further. Emerging fields such as behavioral finance, digital economics, and data-driven econometrics hold great promise for expanding our understanding of economic behavior, financial markets, and policy-making. The integration of artificial intelligence and machine learning into economic analysis is also set to revolutionize the field, enabling more accurate forecasting and policy simulations.

In this chapter, we have explored the evolution of traditional economics from its classical origins to its modern-day manifestations. We have seen how economic theories and paradigms have adapted to address new challenges, incorporate interdisciplinary perspectives, and strive for a more comprehensive understanding of the complex global economy. In the following chapters, we will delve into the impact of cryptocurrency and blockchain technology on traditional economic systems and explore their potential to reshape the world of finance and commerce.

Chapter 3: The Impact of Crypto on Financial Markets

The emergence of cryptocurrencies has had a profound impact on financial markets worldwide. In this chapter, we will explore how crypto has disrupted traditional financial systems, transformed investment landscapes, and revolutionized the way we perceive and engage with money.

3.1 Cryptocurrencies: A New Asset Class

Cryptocurrencies, such as Bitcoin and Ethereum, have introduced a new asset class to the financial markets. Unlike traditional stocks, bonds, or commodities, cryptocurrencies operate on decentralized networks, utilizing blockchain technology. Their unique properties, including limited supply, transparency, and security, have attracted investors seeking alternative investment opportunities.

3.2 Increased Accessibility and Financial Inclusion

One of the significant impacts of crypto on financial markets is increased accessibility. Traditional financial systems often exclude individuals without access to banking services or stringent regulatory requirements. Cryptocurrencies offer a borderless and inclusive financial ecosystem, empowering individuals to participate in the global economy without intermediaries. This has the potential to enhance financial inclusion and bridge economic gaps worldwide.

3.3 Disintermediation and Peer-to-Peer Transactions

Cryptocurrencies enable peer-to-peer transactions without the need for intermediaries like banks or payment processors. By leveraging blockchain technology, individuals can transact directly, reducing costs, eliminating delays, and increasing transparency. This disintermediation has the potential to disrupt traditional financial institutions and reshape the way transactions are conducted.

3.4 Smart Contracts and Decentralized Finance (DeFi)

The integration of smart contracts with cryptocurrencies has given rise to decentralized finance, or DeFi. Smart contracts are self-executing agreements that automatically enforce the terms written within them. DeFi applications built on blockchain platforms enable a wide range of financial activities, such as lending, borrowing, and trading, without the need for intermediaries. This opens up new possibilities for financial innovation, efficiency, and accessibility.

3.5 Liquidity and Global Trading

Cryptocurrencies have introduced unprecedented liquidity to financial markets. Trading pairs between cryptocurrencies and fiat currencies, as well as cryptocurrency-to-cryptocurrency trading, take place on various digital exchanges worldwide. This 24/7 global trading environment offers liquidity and opportunities for investors, allowing them to diversify their portfolios beyond traditional assets and access markets that were previously inaccessible.

3.6 Volatility and Speculation

The crypto market is known for its volatility, with prices often experiencing significant fluctuations in short periods. While volatility presents risks, it also creates opportunities for traders and speculators to profit. Cryptocurrencies have attracted a new breed of investors who thrive in this dynamic environment and actively engage in short-term trading strategies.

3.7 Regulatory Challenges and Market Stability

The impact of crypto on financial markets has posed regulatory challenges for governments and regulatory bodies worldwide. Due to the decentralized and borderless nature of cryptocurrencies, enforcing consistent regulations has proven complex. Regulators aim to strike a balance between fostering innovation, protecting investors, and ensuring market stability. Regulatory frameworks are evolving to address concerns such as money laundering, fraud, and market manipulation.

3.8 Institutional Adoption and Mainstream Recognition

In recent years, cryptocurrencies have gained increased institutional adoption and mainstream recognition. Traditional financial institutions, including banks, asset management firms, and hedge funds, are exploring ways to incorporate cryptocurrencies into their portfolios. The entry of institutional investors has brought more liquidity, stability, and credibility to the crypto market, signaling a maturing industry.

3.9 The Future of Financial Markets with Crypto

As cryptocurrencies continue to evolve, their impact on financial markets is set to expand. The integration of blockchain technology, tokenization of assets, and the potential for central bank digital currencies (CBDCs) will shape the future of finance. Increased regulatory clarity, scalability solutions, and advancements in security and privacy will drive mainstream adoption and further bridge the gap between traditional and crypto-based financial systems.

In this chapter, we have explored how cryptocurrencies have disrupted financial markets, provided increased accessibility and financial inclusion, facilitated peer-to-peer transactions, and introduced new financial instruments such as smart contracts and DeFi. We have also examined the challenges posed by volatility and regulatory complexities, as well as the growing institutional adoption and mainstream recognition of cryptocurrencies. The next chapters will delve deeper into the mechanisms of blockchain technology, the socio-economic impact of crypto, and the potential future scenarios where cryptocurrencies play a central role in reshaping global financial systems.

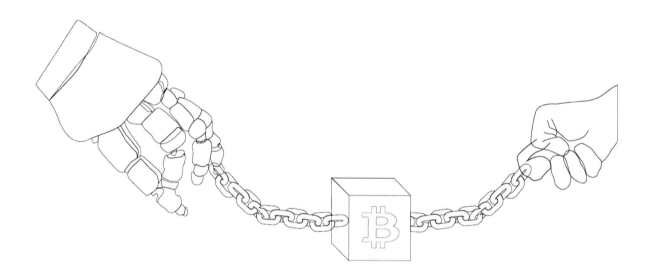

Chapter 4: Blockchain Technology: A Game Changer

Blockchain technology, the underlying foundation of cryptocurrencies, has emerged as a transformative force with the potential to revolutionize various industries beyond finance. In this chapter, we will explore the fundamentals of blockchain, its key features, and the wide-ranging impact it has on sectors such as supply chain management, healthcare, and governance.

4.1 Understanding Blockchain Technology

At its core, blockchain is a decentralized and immutable digital ledger that records transactions across multiple computers, or nodes. Each transaction, or block, is linked to the previous one, forming a chain of information. This distributed and transparent nature of blockchain offers numerous benefits, such as increased security, transparency, and efficiency.

4.2 Decentralization and Trust

One of the key features of blockchain is decentralization. Unlike traditional systems that rely on a central authority, blockchain operates through a network of nodes that collectively validate and maintain the integrity of the ledger. This decentralized approach enhances trust by eliminating the need to rely on a single entity and reducing the risk of fraud or manipulation.

4.3 Immutable and Transparent Transactions

Once a transaction is recorded on the blockchain, it becomes virtually immutable. It cannot be altered or tampered with without the consensus of the majority of network participants. This immutability ensures the integrity of the data, making blockchain a highly secure and reliable technology for storing and transferring value. Additionally, the transparent nature of blockchain allows anyone with access to the network to view transaction histories, promoting accountability and auditability.

4.4 Supply Chain Management and Traceability

Blockchain technology has the potential to revolutionize supply chain management by enabling end-to-end traceability and transparency. By recording every transaction and movement of goods on the blockchain, stakeholders can easily track the origin, authenticity, and journey of products. This helps reduce counterfeiting, ensure compliance with regulations, and enhance consumer trust in the supply chain.

4.5 Transforming Healthcare Systems

In the healthcare sector, blockchain technology holds promise in areas such as electronic health records (EHRs), medical research, and pharmaceutical supply chains. Blockchain-based EHRs provide a secure and interoperable way to store and share patient data, improving data accuracy and patient privacy. Furthermore, blockchain enables transparent and auditable clinical trials, ensuring the integrity of research data. In pharmaceutical supply chains, blockchain enhances drug traceability, reducing the risk of counterfeit medications.

4.6 Enhancing Digital Identity and Authentication

Blockchain technology offers a solution to the challenges associated with digital identity management. Through self-sovereign identity systems, individuals can maintain control over their personal data while securely verifying their identity for various online services. Blockchain-based authentication mechanisms enhance privacy, reduce the risk of identity theft, and streamline digital interactions.

4.7 Governance and Voting Systems

Blockchain has the potential to transform governance and voting systems by introducing transparency, immutability, and increased participation. Through blockchain-based voting platforms, citizens can securely cast their votes, ensuring transparency and preventing tampering. Smart contracts on the blockchain can automate the execution of predefined rules, reducing bureaucracy and enhancing efficiency in government processes.

4.8 Challenges and Scalability

Despite its potential, blockchain technology faces challenges such as scalability, energy consumption, and regulatory frameworks. The current limitations of blockchain networks, such as transaction speed and throughput, hinder their widespread adoption for high-volume applications. However, ongoing research and development aim to address these challenges through advancements like layer 2 solutions, interoperability protocols, and consensus algorithm improvements.

4.9: The Future of Blockchain Technology

The transformative potential of blockchain technology is vast, and its impact on various industries is still unfolding. As the technology continues to mature, we can expect to witness increased adoption, further innovation, and the emergence of new use cases. Integration with emerging technologies such as artificial intelligence, the Internet of Things, and decentralized finance (DeFi) will unlock new possibilities and reshape business models across sectors.

In this chapter, we have explored the fundamental aspects of blockchain technology, its features of decentralization, immutability, and transparency, and the transformative impact it has on supply chain management, healthcare, digital identity, and governance. As blockchain technology continues to evolve, the subsequent chapters will delve deeper into the interaction between blockchain and cryptocurrencies, the challenges and opportunities of decentralized finance, and the potential future scenarios where blockchain becomes an integral part of our daily lives.

Chapter 5: Cryptocurrency and Global Trade

Cryptocurrencies have begun to make their mark in the realm of global trade, offering new possibilities and transforming traditional methods of conducting international business. In this chapter, we will explore the impact of cryptocurrencies on global trade, including cross-border transactions, international payments, and the potential for economic growth and financial inclusion.

5.1 Cross-Border Transactions and Cost Efficiency

Global trade often involves complex and time-consuming cross-border transactions. Cryptocurrencies provide an alternative that simplifies and accelerates these processes. With cryptocurrencies, international transactions can occur directly between parties without the need for intermediaries, reducing costs associated with traditional banking systems, foreign exchange conversion, and international wire transfers. This cost efficiency benefits businesses of all sizes, from multinational corporations to small and medium enterprises (SMEs).

5.2 Enhanced Speed and Accessibility

The use of cryptocurrencies in global trade also improves transaction speed and accessibility. Traditional international payments can take days or even weeks to settle, involving multiple intermediaries and clearance processes. Cryptocurrencies, on the other hand, enable near-instantaneous transactions, eliminating delays and enabling faster trade execution. This increased speed enhances business efficiency and enables agile responses to changing market conditions.

5.3 Mitigating Currency Risks and Volatility

Global trade often involves dealing with multiple currencies, exposing businesses to currency risks and exchange rate volatility. Cryptocurrencies provide a potential solution by enabling direct conversion between different cryptocurrencies or between cryptocurrencies and fiat currencies. This reduces reliance on traditional currency exchange mechanisms, mitigates currency risks, and allows businesses to manage their exposure to market fluctuations more effectively.

5.4 Financial Inclusion and Emerging Markets

Cryptocurrencies have the potential to promote financial inclusion, particularly in emerging markets where access to traditional banking services may be limited. With just a smartphone and internet connectivity, individuals and businesses in underserved regions can participate in global trade by utilizing cryptocurrencies. This opens up new opportunities for economic growth, reduces barriers to entry, and fosters entrepreneurship and innovation in developing economies.

5.5 Smart Contracts and Trade Automation

The integration of cryptocurrencies with smart contracts introduces a new level of automation and efficiency in global trade. Smart contracts are self-executing agreements that automatically trigger actions based on predefined conditions. In trade, smart contracts can facilitate processes such as supply chain management, automated payments, and trade financing, reducing paperwork, streamlining operations, and increasing trust between parties.

5.6 Transparency and Trust in Global Trade

Blockchain technology, the underlying technology of cryptocurrencies, offers transparency and trust in global trade. Blockchain-based supply chain solutions enable businesses to track and verify the origin, authenticity, and movement of goods throughout the entire supply chain. This transparency enhances trust between trading partners, reduces the risk of counterfeit products, and strengthens consumer confidence.

5.7 Regulatory and Legal Considerations

As cryptocurrencies gain traction in global trade, regulatory and legal frameworks are evolving to address the unique challenges and opportunities they present. Governments and international bodies are exploring ways to strike a balance between fostering innovation and ensuring consumer protection, cybersecurity, and anti-money laundering measures. Regulatory clarity and international cooperation are essential for the widespread adoption of cryptocurrencies in global trade.

5.8. Challenges and Future Outlook

Despite the potential benefits, challenges remain in integrating cryptocurrencies into global trade. Scalability, regulatory complexities, and concerns about price volatility and security require ongoing attention and development. However, as technological advancements, industry collaboration, and regulatory frameworks progress, cryptocurrencies are likely to play an increasingly significant role in shaping the future of global trade.

In this chapter, we have explored how cryptocurrencies are transforming global trade by enhancing cost efficiency, speed, accessibility, and financial inclusion. We have also discussed the potential of smart contracts, blockchain-based supply chain solutions, and the importance of transparency and trust in international trade. As the integration of cryptocurrencies continues to evolve, the subsequent chapters will delve deeper into their impact on financial markets, the challenges and opportunities of decentralized finance, and the potential future scenarios where cryptocurrencies become a mainstream medium of exchange in the global economy.

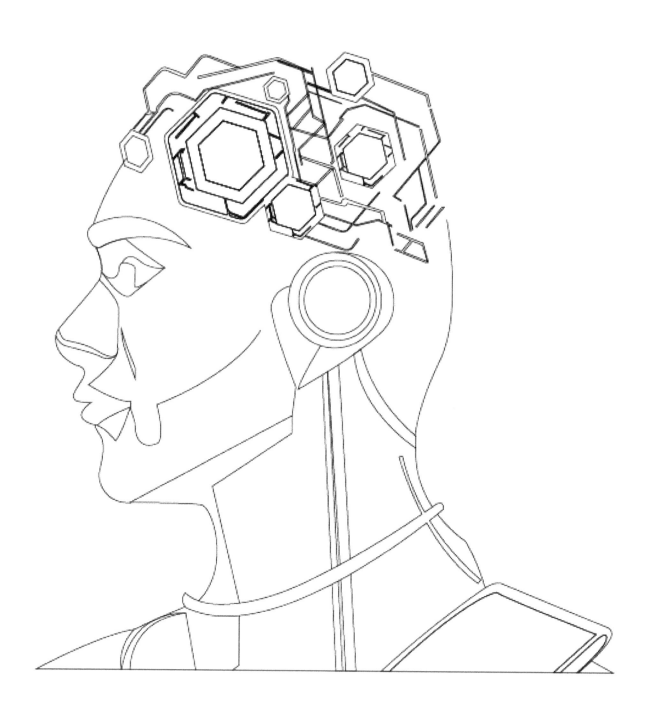

Chapter 6: Decentralization: Empowering Individuals

Decentralization lies at the heart of cryptocurrencies and blockchain technology, revolutionizing the way power and control are distributed in various aspects of our lives. In this chapter, we will explore how decentralization empowers individuals by providing greater autonomy, fostering innovation, and challenging traditional centralized systems.

6.1 Understanding Decentralization

Decentralization refers to the distribution of power, authority, and decision-making across a network rather than being concentrated in a single central entity or authority. In the context of cryptocurrencies, decentralization eliminates the need for intermediaries such as banks or governments to oversee and control transactions. Instead, transactions are verified, recorded, and maintained by a decentralized network of participants.

6.2 Autonomy and Ownership of Assets

Decentralization empowers individuals by granting them greater autonomy and ownership of their assets. With cryptocurrencies, individuals have direct control over their digital wallets and private keys, allowing them to transact and manage their funds without relying on traditional financial intermediaries. This autonomy provides a sense of ownership and control over one's financial resources.

6.3 Financial Inclusion and Economic Empowerment

Decentralization plays a pivotal role in promoting financial inclusion and economic empowerment. Traditional financial systems often exclude individuals without access to banking services or those living in economically disadvantaged regions. Cryptocurrencies offer a decentralized financial ecosystem, enabling individuals to participate in the global economy, access financial services, and engage in economic activities. This inclusivity can uplift marginalized communities and drive economic growth.

6.4 Disintermediation and Peer-to-Peer Transactions

Decentralization removes the need for intermediaries, enabling direct peer-to-peer transactions. This disintermediation has significant implications for various industries beyond finance. For instance, decentralized marketplaces can connect buyers and sellers directly, eliminating the need for intermediaries such as e-commerce platforms. This fosters a more equitable and efficient exchange of goods and services, empowering individuals to engage in direct trade.

6.5 Transparency and Trust

Blockchain-based, decentralized systems offer transparency and enhanced trust. Transactions recorded on the blockchain are visible to all participants, ensuring transparency and accountability. This transparency reduces the need to blindly trust intermediaries or centralized authorities. Instead, trust is established through the consensus mechanism and cryptographic protocols of the blockchain network, fostering a more trustless and secure environment for individuals to transact and interact.

6.6 Innovation and Collaboration

Decentralization encourages innovation and collaboration by lowering barriers to entry. In centralized systems, innovation often requires approval from gatekeepers or adherence to established protocols. Decentralized platforms and open-source projects provide fertile ground for developers, entrepreneurs, and creative individuals to contribute, innovate, and build upon existing technologies. This fosters a culture of collaboration, enabling the collective wisdom of the community to drive progress.

6.7 Censorship Resistance and Freedom of Expression

Centralized systems can exert control over information and limit freedom of expression. Decentralization challenges this by offering censorship resistance. Blockchain-based platforms can provide immutable and censorship-resistant systems for content sharing, social media, and communication. This empowers individuals to express their opinions freely without fear of censorship, ensuring a more open and democratic exchange of ideas.

6.8 Challenges and Considerations

While decentralization brings significant benefits, challenges exist in its implementation. Scalability, energy consumption, regulatory frameworks, and the potential for misuse require careful consideration. Striking a balance between decentralization, user protections, and societal norms is an ongoing process that necessitates collaboration between technologists, regulators, and stakeholders.

6.9: The Future of Decentralization

Decentralization has the potential to reshape various aspects of our society, from finance and governance to communication and beyond. As technology evolves and blockchain applications mature, the vision of a decentralized future becomes more tangible. Continued exploration, research, and responsible development will unlock new possibilities and empower individuals to participate actively in shaping their own destinies.

In this chapter, we have explored the empowering nature of decentralization, which grants individuals autonomy, financial inclusion, and ownership of assets. We discussed the potential for disintermediation, transparency, trust, and collaboration that decentralization brings. While challenges exist, the future holds immense potential for decentralization to empower individuals and redefine the structures of power in our society. In the subsequent chapters, we will delve deeper into the interplay between cryptocurrencies and decentralized systems, the impact on traditional institutions, and the potential for decentralized finance to reshape the financial landscape.

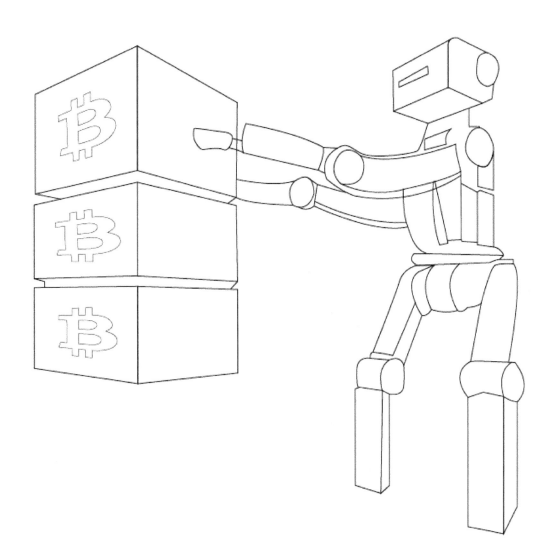

Chapter 7: Challenges and Opportunities in the Crypto Space

The crypto space has experienced rapid growth and garnered significant attention in recent years. Alongside the opportunities presented by cryptocurrencies and blockchain technology, there are also various challenges that need to be addressed. In this chapter, we will explore the challenges and opportunities that exist within the crypto space.

7.1 Volatility and Price Fluctuations

One of the primary challenges in the crypto space is the high volatility and price fluctuations experienced by cryptocurrencies. The values of cryptocurrencies can fluctuate significantly within short periods, presenting risks and uncertainties for investors and users. Price volatility can be attributed to factors such as market speculation, regulatory developments, technological advancements, and macroeconomic trends. Managing and mitigating this volatility is a challenge that requires careful risk assessment and strategic decision-making.

7.2 Regulatory Environment and Uncertainty

The regulatory landscape surrounding cryptocurrencies remains complex and uncertain in many jurisdictions. Governments and regulatory bodies are grappling with how to regulate and oversee this rapidly evolving space. Divergent approaches to regulation globally create challenges for individuals, businesses, and exchanges operating across borders. Achieving a balance between fostering innovation and safeguarding consumer protection, anti-money laundering measures, and financial stability is crucial for the sustainable growth of the crypto space.

7.3 Security and Custody of Assets

Security is a critical concern in the crypto space due to the prevalence of hacking attempts and cybersecurity threats. Ensuring the safe storage and custody of cryptocurrency assets is of paramount importance. Cryptocurrency exchanges, wallets, and other service providers must implement robust security measures, including multi-factor authentication, encryption, and cold storage solutions, to protect users' funds. The challenge lies in staying ahead of ever-evolving security threats and providing a secure environment for users.

7.4 Scalability and Network Congestion

Scalability is a significant challenge in the crypto space, particularly for blockchain networks. As the number of users and transactions grows, congestion on the network can occur, leading to slower transaction speeds and higher fees. This poses challenges for the widespread adoption and scalability of blockchain-based applications. Solutions such as layer 2 protocols, sharding, and advancements in consensus mechanisms are being explored to address these scalability issues.

7.5 User Experience and Education

Improving the user experience and educating the public about cryptocurrencies and blockchain technology are essential for broader adoption. The complexity of the technology, lack of user-friendly interfaces, and unfamiliarity with crypto-related concepts can create barriers for newcomers. Simplifying the onboarding process, enhancing user interfaces, and providing educational resources are opportunities to bridge the gap and make cryptocurrencies more accessible to a wider audience.

7.6 Financial Inclusion and Emerging Markets

Cryptocurrencies have the potential to promote financial inclusion, particularly in emerging markets where access to traditional banking services is limited. However, challenges such as technological barriers, connectivity issues, and regulatory hurdles must be addressed to fully unlock this potential. Opportunities lie in developing user-friendly wallets, expanding access to digital infrastructure, and working with regulators to establish appropriate frameworks that foster innovation while protecting consumers.

7.7 Decentralized Finance (DeFi) and Innovation

DeFi represents a rapidly growing sector within the crypto space, offering opportunities for innovative financial products and services. The ability to borrow, lend, trade, and earn interest without relying on traditional intermediaries has the potential to reshape the financial landscape. However, the nascent nature of DeFi also brings challenges related to smart contract security, regulatory compliance, and the need for robust risk management practices.

7.8. Interoperability and Standardization

Interoperability and standardization are critical for the seamless integration of different blockchain networks and crypto ecosystems. Achieving interoperability would allow for the efficient transfer of assets and data across disparate systems, foster collaboration, and expand use cases. Establishing common standards and protocols is an opportunity for the crypto space to mature and create a more interconnected and interoperable ecosystem.

7.9 Environmental Impact and Sustainability

The energy consumption associated with some cryptocurrencies, particularly Bitcoin, has raised concerns about their environmental impact. The opportunity lies in developing and adopting more sustainable consensus mechanisms and energy-efficient technologies. Initiatives focusing on renewable energy sources, carbon offsetting, and responsible mining practices can contribute to a greener and more sustainable crypto space.

In this chapter, we have explored the challenges and opportunities present in the crypto space. From volatility and regulatory uncertainties to security, scalability, and user experience, the crypto industry faces various hurdles that need to be overcome. However, these challenges also provide opportunities for innovation, financial inclusion, and the reshaping of traditional systems. By addressing these challenges and embracing the opportunities, the crypto space can evolve and mature, unlocking its full potential for the benefit of individuals and society at large.

Chapter 8: The Role of AI in Crypto Research

Artificial Intelligence (AI) has emerged as a powerful tool with the potential to revolutionize various industries, including the field of cryptocurrency research. In this chapter, we will explore the role of AI in crypto research, its applications, and the impact it has on enhancing market analysis, risk assessment, and investment strategies.

8.1 Introduction to AI in Crypto Research

AI encompasses a range of technologies, including machine learning, natural language processing, and data analytics, that enable computers to perform tasks that traditionally required human intelligence. In the realm of crypto research, AI offers the ability to analyze vast amounts of data, detect patterns, and derive valuable insights, facilitating informed decision-making and strategy development.

8.2 Market Analysis and Price Prediction

AI plays a vital role in market analysis by processing and analyzing large volumes of historical and real-time data from cryptocurrency markets. Machine learning algorithms can identify patterns, correlations, and anomalies, enabling the prediction of price movements and market trends. AI-powered models help traders and investors make informed decisions by providing insights into potential market opportunities and risks.

8.3: Sentiment Analysis and Social Media Monitoring

AI can analyze social media platforms, news articles, and forums to gauge market sentiment and public perception of cryptocurrencies. Sentiment analysis algorithms can process textual data and extract insights to understand public sentiment, helping traders and investors assess market sentiment and make informed decisions. Monitoring social media also aids in identifying emerging trends, sentiment shifts, and potential market manipulations.

8.4 Risk Assessment and Fraud Detection

AI algorithms can assist in risk assessment by analyzing transactional data to identify suspicious activities and potential fraud. Machine learning models can detect patterns indicative of fraudulent behavior, such as money laundering or market manipulation, enhancing security and mitigating risks in the crypto space. By identifying high-risk transactions or addresses, AI helps maintain the integrity of the blockchain ecosystem.

8.5 Portfolio Management and Investment Strategies

AI-powered portfolio management systems utilize advanced algorithms to optimize investment strategies. By considering factors such as risk tolerance, investment goals, and market conditions, AI can recommend diversified portfolios and allocation strategies tailored to individual investors. These systems can continuously monitor and adjust portfolios based on real-time market data, ensuring optimal performance and risk management.

8.6 Algorithmic Trading and Execution

AI enables the development of sophisticated algorithmic trading systems that execute trades based on predefined rules and strategies. Machine learning algorithms can analyze market data, identify trading signals, and execute trades with speed and precision. AI-driven trading systems can remove emotional biases, capitalize on market inefficiencies, and improve trading execution, enhancing overall trading performance.

8.7 Enhancing Security and Anti-Money Laundering (AML) Compliance

AI technologies assist in enhancing security in the crypto space by detecting and preventing fraudulent activities. Machine learning algorithms can analyze transactional patterns, detect anomalies, and flag suspicious activities for further investigation. Additionally, AI-powered systems aid in ensuring compliance with anti-money laundering regulations by monitoring transactions, identifying potential risks, and providing automated reporting mechanisms.

8.8 Improving Blockchain Governance and Consensus Mechanisms

AI has the potential to enhance blockchain governance by enabling more efficient consensus mechanisms. Machine learning algorithms can optimize consensus protocols, improve network performance, and address scalability challenges. AI-driven governance models can provide more inclusive decision-making processes, automate voting mechanisms, and foster consensus among network participants.

8.9 Challenges and Ethical Considerations

While AI offers significant benefits to crypto research, challenges and ethical considerations must be addressed. Ensuring data privacy, avoiding biases in AI models, and considering the potential impact of AI on market dynamics are crucial. Striking a balance between AI automation and human expertise is essential to maintaining transparency, accountability, and responsible decision-making.

In this chapter, we have explored the role of AI in crypto research, highlighting its applications in market analysis, price prediction, sentiment analysis, risk assessment, and portfolio management. AI's ability to process vast amounts of data, detect patterns, and provide valuable insights contributes to informed decision-making and enhances strategies in the crypto space. However, it is important to recognize the challenges and ethical considerations associated with AI adoption. The subsequent chapters will delve deeper into the interaction between AI and blockchain technology and the potential future scenarios where these technologies collaborate to reshape various industries, including finance and beyond.

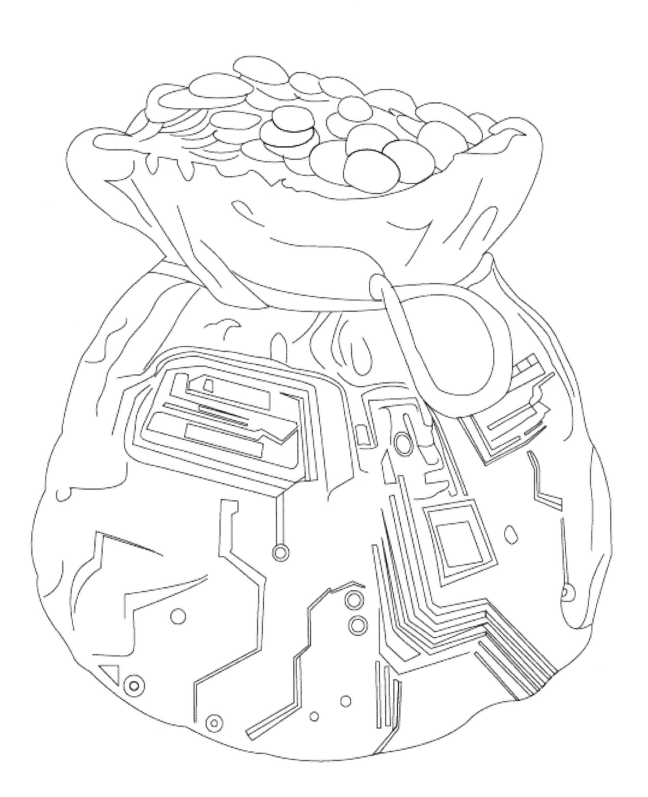

Chapter 9: Smart Contracts: Automating Transactions

Smart contracts have emerged as a powerful application of blockchain technology, enabling the automation and execution of agreements without the need for intermediaries. In this chapter, we will explore the concept of smart contracts, their benefits, and their impact on automating transactions across various industries.

9.1 Understanding Smart Contracts

Smart contracts are self-executing contracts with the terms of the agreement directly written into lines of code. These contracts are stored and executed on a blockchain network, ensuring transparency, security, and immutability. Smart contracts automate the enforcement and execution of agreements, removing the need for intermediaries and reducing human intervention.

9.2 Benefits of Smart Contracts

Smart contracts offer numerous benefits over traditional contractual arrangements. Firstly, they eliminate the need for intermediaries, such as lawyers or brokers, reducing costs and potential conflicts of interest. Secondly, smart contracts provide transparency, as all parties involved can access and verify the terms of the contract on the blockchain. Additionally, smart contracts are tamper-proof and immutable, ensuring the integrity of the agreement. Finally, the automation of contract execution streamlines processes, reduces manual errors, and enables faster transactions.

9.3 Use Cases of Smart Contracts

Smart contracts have a wide range of use cases across industries. In finance, they can automate payments, facilitate crowdfunding campaigns, and enable decentralized lending and borrowing. In supply chain management, smart contracts can automate the tracking and verification of goods, ensuring transparency and reducing fraud. Real estate transactions, insurance claims, and intellectual property rights management are also areas where smart contracts can streamline processes and enhance efficiency.

9.4 Technical Aspects of Smart Contracts

Smart contracts are written in programming languages specifically designed for the blockchain, such as Solidity for Ethereum. These contracts consist of a code that defines the rules and conditions of the agreement. Once deployed on the blockchain, smart contracts are executed automatically when the predefined conditions are met. Smart contracts can interact with other smart contracts, access data on the blockchain, and trigger actions based on external events.

9.5 Oracles and External Data

Smart contracts can be limited in their ability to directly access external data sources. Oracles act as intermediaries, providing smart contracts with real-world data such as stock prices, weather conditions, or IoT device readings. Oracles enable smart contracts to interact with off-chain data, expanding their use cases and enabling more complex agreements.

9.6 Challenges and Considerations

While smart contracts offer significant advantages, challenges exist that need to be addressed. One challenge is the complexity of writing secure and bug-free code, as vulnerabilities in smart contracts can lead to costly exploits. Auditing and testing procedures are essential to mitigating these risks. Additionally, legal frameworks and regulatory compliance issues surrounding smart contracts are still evolving, requiring adaptation to ensure their enforceability.

9.7 Evolving Smart Contract Platforms

Smart contract platforms, such as Ethereum, are continuously evolving to address scalability, speed, and energy consumption concerns. Upgrades like Ethereum 2.0 aim to enhance scalability and reduce transaction costs. Other platforms, such as Cardano and Polkadot, offer alternative approaches to smart contract execution, aiming to improve performance and interoperability.

9.8. The Future of Smart Contracts

The potential of smart contracts is vast, and their adoption is likely to expand further as blockchain technology matures. The integration of smart contracts with emerging technologies such as the Internet of Things, artificial intelligence, and decentralized finance (DeFi) will unlock new possibilities and reshape business processes across industries. As smart contract platforms evolve and regulatory frameworks adapt, smart contracts will become increasingly integrated into our daily lives.

In this chapter, we have explored the concept of smart contracts and their benefits in automating transactions. We discussed their advantages over traditional contracts, the technical aspects involved, and the challenges and considerations surrounding their implementation. Smart contracts have the potential to revolutionize various industries by streamlining processes, reducing costs, and increasing transparency. As the technology advances, the subsequent chapters will delve deeper into the interaction between smart contracts, blockchain, and other emerging technologies, exploring their combined impact on reshaping industries and fostering new opportunities.

Chapter 10: Cryptocurrency and Financial Inclusion

Cryptocurrencies have the potential to foster financial inclusion by providing access to financial services for individuals and communities that are underserved or excluded from traditional banking systems. In this chapter, we will explore how cryptocurrencies promote financial inclusion, empower individuals, and create opportunities for economic growth and empowerment.

10.1 Barriers to Financial Inclusion

Traditional banking systems often impose barriers to financial inclusion, leaving a significant portion of the global population without access to basic financial services. Factors such as geographical limitations, a lack of documentation, high transaction fees, and minimum deposit requirements restrict individuals from participating in the formal financial system. This exclusion perpetuates socioeconomic inequalities and hinders economic development.

10.2 Empowering the Unbanked and Underbanked

Cryptocurrencies have the potential to empower the unbanked and underbanked populations by providing them with an alternative financial ecosystem. With just a smartphone and internet access, individuals can participate in the global economy, access financial services, and engage in economic activities. Cryptocurrencies remove the need for traditional intermediaries, enabling direct peer-to-peer transactions, eliminating geographical barriers, and reducing costs associated with banking services.

10.3 Remittances and Cross-Border Payments

Remittances play a crucial role in the global economy, particularly in developing countries where individuals rely on funds sent from abroad. Cryptocurrencies offer a faster and more cost-effective solution for cross-border remittances compared to traditional remittance methods. By leveraging cryptocurrencies, individuals can send and receive funds instantly and at a fraction of the cost, enhancing the efficiency and accessibility of remittance services.

10.4 Microtransactions and Microlending

Cryptocurrencies facilitate microtransactions, enabling the transfer of small amounts of value without incurring high transaction fees. This opens up opportunities for individuals in low-income communities to engage in economic activities such as microentrepreneurship and microwork, where small transactions are common. Additionally, cryptocurrencies enable microlending platforms, connecting lenders directly with borrowers without the need for traditional financial intermediaries.

10.5 Access to Savings and Investment Opportunities

Cryptocurrencies provide access to savings and investment opportunities for individuals who may not have access to traditional banking services. By holding cryptocurrencies, individuals can store value, protect their wealth, and participate in investment opportunities. Decentralized finance (DeFi) platforms built on blockchain technology offer a range of financial instruments, including lending, borrowing, and yield farming, which can generate income and grow wealth.

10.6 Financial Education and Literacy

Promoting financial inclusion goes hand in hand with financial education and literacy. Cryptocurrencies provide an opportunity to educate individuals about basic financial concepts, digital literacy, and the responsible use of cryptocurrencies. Empowering individuals with knowledge and skills enhances their ability to make informed financial decisions, protect their assets, and navigate the crypto ecosystem safely.

10.7 Regulatory Considerations

As cryptocurrencies gain traction in promoting financial inclusion, regulatory frameworks must be developed to protect consumers, ensure compliance with anti-money laundering regulations, and safeguard against fraudulent activities. Regulations that strike a balance between fostering innovation and protecting individuals are necessary to maintain the integrity of the financial system and promote trust in cryptocurrencies.

10.8. Partnerships and Collaboration

Promoting financial inclusion through cryptocurrencies requires partnerships and collaboration between various stakeholders. Governments, financial institutions, technology companies, and nonprofits can work together to develop infrastructure, establish regulatory frameworks, and provide support services to educate and onboard individuals into the crypto ecosystem. Collaboration enables the pooling of resources and expertise to address the unique challenges and opportunities associated with financial inclusion.

10.9: The Socioeconomic Impact

Cryptocurrencies have the potential to have a significant socioeconomic impact by providing financial inclusion. Increased access to financial services fosters economic growth, reduces poverty, and empowers individuals and communities. By leveraging the opportunities presented by cryptocurrencies, individuals can save, invest, transact, and build financial stability, contributing to their overall well-being and the growth of the global economy.

In this chapter, we have explored how cryptocurrencies promote financial inclusion by empowering the unbanked and underbanked populations. We discussed the opportunities cryptocurrencies provide for remittances, microtransactions, savings, and investments. We also highlighted the importance of financial education, regulatory considerations, and partnerships to ensure responsible and inclusive adoption of cryptocurrencies. The subsequent chapters will delve deeper into the potential impact of cryptocurrencies on traditional financial systems, the challenges and opportunities of decentralized finance, and the potential future scenarios where cryptocurrencies and blockchain technology reshape the global economic landscape.

Chapter 11: Regulatory Frameworks for Crypto

The growing popularity and global reach of cryptocurrencies have prompted governments and regulatory bodies to develop frameworks to address the unique challenges and opportunities presented by this emerging technology. In this chapter, we will explore the importance of regulatory frameworks for cryptocurrencies, the key considerations for regulators, and the potential impact on the crypto industry and its participants.

11.1: The Need for Regulatory Frameworks

Regulatory frameworks play a crucial role in ensuring consumer protection, market integrity, and financial stability in the crypto space. They provide clarity on the legal status of cryptocurrencies, define the obligations and responsibilities of market participants, and establish safeguards against illicit activities such as money laundering, terrorist financing, and fraud. Regulatory frameworks also aim to strike a balance between fostering innovation and protecting investors and consumers.

11.2 Approaches to Cryptocurrency Regulation

Regulatory approaches to cryptocurrencies vary across jurisdictions, reflecting different legal, economic, and cultural contexts. Some countries have adopted a permissive approach, embracing cryptocurrencies and blockchain technology to foster innovation and economic growth. Others have taken a cautious approach, imposing strict regulations to mitigate risks and protect investors. The regulatory landscape is continually evolving as governments and regulators adapt to the unique challenges posed by cryptocurrencies.

11.3 Key Considerations for Regulators

When developing regulatory frameworks for cryptocurrencies, regulators must consider various factors. These include investor protection, consumer education, market transparency, anti-money laundering (AML) and know-your-customer (KYC) requirements, tax implications, custody and security standards, and market surveillance. Balancing innovation with risk management is crucial to ensuring that regulatory frameworks are effective, proportionate, and adaptable to the evolving crypto landscape.

11.4 Licensing and Registration Requirements

Many jurisdictions require cryptocurrency businesses, such as exchanges, wallet providers, and custodians, to obtain licenses or register with regulatory authorities. These requirements aim to ensure compliance with regulatory standards, enhance transparency, and provide a level of consumer protection. Licensing frameworks typically involve rigorous due diligence, capital requirements, and ongoing compliance obligations.

11.5 Investor Protection and Consumer Safeguards

Regulatory frameworks aim to protect investors and consumers by setting standards for market conduct, disclosure requirements, and dispute resolution mechanisms. Regulators often require crypto businesses to implement robust AML and KYC procedures, conduct customer due diligence, and maintain adequate security measures to safeguard user funds.

Education initiatives and consumer awareness campaigns also play a crucial role in empowering individuals to make informed decisions and protect themselves.

11.6 International Cooperation and Harmonization

Cryptocurrencies operate across borders, making international cooperation and harmonization of regulatory approaches essential. Collaboration between regulatory authorities and international organizations facilitates information sharing, coordination of enforcement actions, and the development of consistent regulatory standards. Global initiatives such as the Financial Action Task Force (FATF) provide guidance on AML and counter-terrorism financing measures, helping create a cohesive global regulatory environment.

11.7 Impact on Innovation and Market Development

Regulatory frameworks have a profound impact on the innovation and development of the crypto industry. Well-designed regulations can provide clarity and certainty, attract investment, and foster innovation. However, excessive or unclear regulations may stifle innovation and drive businesses to more favorable jurisdictions. Striking the right balance between regulation and innovation is crucial to ensuring that regulatory frameworks support the growth of the crypto industry.

11.8 Emerging Regulatory Trends

Regulatory trends in the crypto space include the implementation of comprehensive licensing regimes, increased scrutiny of initial coin offerings (ICOs), the development of regulatory sandboxes to foster innovation, and the introduction of stricter AML and KYC requirements. Regulatory frameworks are also adapting to address decentralized finance (DeFi), stablecoins, and other emerging areas within the crypto industry.

11.9 Continued Evolution of Regulatory Frameworks

Regulatory frameworks for cryptocurrencies are continually evolving as regulators gain a deeper understanding of the technology and its implications. Ongoing dialogue and collaboration between regulators, industry participants, and other stakeholders are vital to developing effective and adaptable frameworks. Regulators must remain responsive to market developments, emerging risks, and the evolving needs of the crypto industry.

In this chapter, we have explored the importance of regulatory frameworks for cryptocurrencies and their impact on investor protection, market integrity, and financial stability. We discussed the key considerations for regulators: licensing and registration requirements, investor protection measures, international cooperation, and the impact on innovation and market development. As the crypto industry continues to grow, regulatory frameworks will play a crucial role in shaping its future, ensuring responsible and sustainable development while balancing innovation and risk management.

Chapter 12: Investing in Cryptocurrency: Risks and Rewards

Investing in cryptocurrency has gained significant popularity as digital assets continue to disrupt traditional financial markets. While it offers the potential for substantial rewards, it also carries inherent risks. In this chapter, we will explore the risks and rewards associated with investing in cryptocurrency, providing insights to help investors make informed decisions.

12.1 Volatility and Price Fluctuations

One of the primary characteristics of the cryptocurrency market is its high volatility and price fluctuations. Cryptocurrencies can experience significant price swings within short periods, driven by market speculation, regulatory developments, technological advancements, and macroeconomic factors. This volatility presents both opportunities and risks for investors, as it can result in substantial gains or losses.

12.2 Market and Liquidity Risks

The cryptocurrency market is relatively nascent and less liquid compared to traditional financial markets. This illiquidity can pose challenges when it comes to buying and selling assets, particularly during periods of market stress. Additionally, the lack of regulation and oversight in certain jurisdictions can increase the risk of market manipulation, fraud, and security breaches. Investors should carefully consider the market dynamics and associated risks before entering the cryptocurrency market.

12.3 Cybersecurity and Hacking Risks

The decentralized nature of cryptocurrencies makes them an attractive target for cybercriminals. Hacking incidents, thefts, and exchange breaches have occurred in the past, resulting in significant losses for investors. Securing digital assets in wallets and employing robust security measures, such as two-factor authentication and cold storage, can help mitigate these risks. However, investors should remain vigilant and stay informed about the latest security practices to protect their investments.

12.4 Regulatory and Legal Risks

Cryptocurrency regulations vary across jurisdictions, and the regulatory landscape is continually evolving. Changes in regulations can impact the value and legality of cryptocurrencies, affecting investor sentiment and market dynamics. Investors should stay informed about the regulatory environment and consider the potential implications of regulatory developments for their investments. Compliance with tax obligations and adherence to legal requirements are also crucial considerations for cryptocurrency investors.

12.5 Diversification and Portfolio Management

Diversification is an important risk management strategy for cryptocurrency investors. Spreading investments across different cryptocurrencies, industry sectors, and asset classes can help mitigate the impact of price volatility and reduce the risk of concentrated losses. Moreover, adopting sound portfolio management principles, setting investment goals, and regularly reviewing and rebalancing portfolios are essential practices for long-term success in cryptocurrency investing.

12.6 Market Manipulation and Speculative Behavior

The cryptocurrency market is susceptible to market manipulation and speculative behavior. Pump-and-dump schemes, false information campaigns, and price manipulation tactics can artificially inflate or deflate cryptocurrency prices, leading to significant losses for unsuspecting investors. Conducting thorough research, verifying information from reliable sources, and avoiding impulsive decisions based on market hype are crucial to navigating the market and mitigating the risks of manipulation.

12.7 Opportunities for Growth and Innovation

Despite the risks, investing in cryptocurrency also presents opportunities for growth and innovation. The crypto market has witnessed significant advancements in technology, decentralized finance (DeFi), and blockchain-based applications. Investing in promising projects and technologies can offer substantial returns on investment, especially when coupled with thorough research and analysis and a long-term investment perspective.

12.8 Global Market Accessibility and Financial Inclusion

Cryptocurrencies provide investors with opportunities for global market accessibility and financial inclusion. Individuals in underserved regions, where traditional financial services may be limited, can participate in the crypto market, access investment opportunities, and engage in economic activities. This inclusivity can contribute to economic growth and empower individuals who were previously excluded from traditional financial systems.

12.9: The Importance of Due Diligence and Education

Conducting thorough due diligence and educating oneself about the fundamentals of cryptocurrencies and blockchain technology are crucial for successful investing. Understanding the underlying technology, evaluating project teams, assessing market trends, and staying informed about regulatory developments can help investors make informed decisions and manage risks effectively. Continuous learning and adapting to the evolving crypto landscape are essential for successful cryptocurrency investing.

In this chapter, we have explored the risks and rewards associated with investing in cryptocurrency. The high volatility, market risks, cybersecurity threats, regulatory challenges, and market manipulation risks are important considerations for investors. However, with careful risk management, diversification, and informed decision-making, cryptocurrency investments offer opportunities for growth, innovation, and global market accessibility. As the crypto market evolves, investors should remain diligent, stay informed, and adapt their strategies to navigate the ever-changing landscape of cryptocurrency investing.

Chapter 13: Crypto Mining: Energy Consumption and Sustainability

Crypto mining, the process of validating transactions and adding them to the blockchain, has become a vital component of many cryptocurrencies. However, the energy consumption associated with mining activities has raised concerns about environmental sustainability. In this chapter, we will explore the energy consumption of crypto mining, its environmental impact, and the potential for sustainable mining practices.

13.1 Understanding Cryptomining

Crypto mining involves using computational power to solve complex mathematical puzzles, a process known as proof-of-work (PoW), in order to validate transactions and secure the blockchain network. Miners compete to find the correct solution, and the first miner to solve the puzzle is rewarded with newly minted cryptocurrency. This energy-intensive process requires powerful hardware and significant computational resources.

13.2 Energy Consumption of Crypto Mining

Crypto mining is known for its substantial energy consumption. The mining process requires miners to continuously operate high-powered computer systems, which consume significant amounts of electricity. As the mining difficulty increases and more miners participate, the energy requirements escalate. Cryptocurrencies like Bitcoin, which use the PoW consensus mechanism, have particularly high energy consumption due to the computational power needed to mine new blocks.

13.3 Environmental Impact of Crypto Mining

The environmental impact of crypto mining is primarily associated with the carbon emissions resulting from the energy generation process. The majority of energy sources worldwide rely on fossil fuels, such as coal and natural gas, which release greenhouse gases when burned. The intensive energy consumption of mining operations contributes to carbon emissions and can have negative implications for climate change and air quality.

13.4 Renewable Energy and Sustainable Mining

One approach to addressing the environmental impact of crypto mining is the use of renewable energy sources. Transitioning mining operations to renewable energy sources, such as solar, wind, hydroelectric, or geothermal power, can significantly reduce carbon emissions. Some mining facilities are already utilizing renewable energy to power their operations, demonstrating the potential for sustainable mining practices.

13.5 Energy Efficiency and Optimization

Improving energy efficiency is another avenue for sustainable mining. The development of more energy-efficient mining hardware, such as application-specific integrated circuits (ASICs), has helped reduce energy consumption per unit of computational power. Additionally, optimizing mining algorithms and protocols can contribute to energy savings by streamlining the mining process and reducing computational waste.

13.6 Alternative Consensus Mechanisms

Cryptocurrencies are exploring alternative consensus mechanisms to reduce energy consumption. Proof-of-Stake (PoS), for example, requires users to hold a certain amount of cryptocurrency to validate transactions, eliminating the need for energy-intensive mining. PoS consumes significantly less energy compared to PoW, making it a more sustainable alternative. Transitioning to energy-efficient consensus mechanisms can reduce the environmental impact of crypto mining.

13.7 Regulation and Industry Standards

Regulation and industry standards can play a significant role in promoting sustainable mining practices. Governments and regulatory bodies can incentivize the use of renewable energy, impose carbon offset requirements, or implement guidelines for energy-efficient mining operations. Industry organizations can establish standards and best practices for mining facilities, encouraging the adoption of sustainable energy sources and efficient mining technologies.

13.8 Transparency and Carbon Footprint Reporting

Increasing transparency in the crypto mining industry can help address sustainability concerns. Mining operations can voluntarily disclose their energy consumption and carbon emissions, allowing for the assessment and comparison of their environmental impact. Carbon footprint reporting frameworks specific to the crypto mining sector can be developed to facilitate accountability and promote sustainable practices.

13.9 Community Initiatives and Education

Community initiatives and education are essential for driving change and promoting sustainability in crypto mining. Collaboration among miners, blockchain projects, and environmental organizations can foster the development of sustainable mining practices. Educational efforts can raise awareness about the environmental impact of mining, encourage responsible energy consumption, and inspire the adoption of sustainable solutions.

In this chapter, we have explored the energy consumption of crypto mining and its environmental impact. We discussed the potential for sustainable mining practices through the use of renewable energy, energy efficiency improvements, and alternative consensus mechanisms. We also highlighted the role of regulation, industry standards, transparency, and community initiatives in promoting sustainable mining. By embracing sustainable approaches, the crypto mining industry can strive towards minimizing its carbon footprint and contributing to a more environmentally sustainable future.

Chapter 14: The Future of Money: Central Bank Digital Currencies

Central Bank Digital Currencies (CBDCs) have emerged as a transformative innovation in the realm of money and payments. As digital representations of a nation's currency, CBDCs have the potential to revolutionize financial systems, enhance monetary policy, and reshape the way we transact. In this chapter, we will explore the concept of CBDCs, their benefits, challenges, and potential future implications for the global financial landscape.

14.1 Understanding Central Bank Digital Currencies

Central Bank Digital Currencies are digital representations of a country's fiat currency, issued and regulated by the central bank. Unlike cryptocurrencies, which operate on decentralized networks, CBDCs maintain centralized control by the central bank, ensuring compliance with monetary policies and regulatory frameworks. CBDCs aim to combine the advantages of digital payments with the stability and trust associated with traditional fiat currencies.

14.2 Enhancing Financial Inclusion and Accessibility

CBDCs hold the potential to improve financial inclusion by providing individuals who lack access to traditional banking services with a secure and convenient digital payment infrastructure. CBDCs can enable low-cost and instantaneous peer-to-peer transactions, facilitating financial services for the unbanked and underbanked populations. This inclusivity can contribute to economic growth, reduce poverty, and promote financial empowerment.

14.3 Efficiency and Cost Reductions

The digitization of money through CBDCs can streamline payment systems, making transactions faster, more efficient, and less costly. By eliminating the need for intermediaries, such as clearinghouses and payment processors, CBDCs can reduce transaction fees and processing times. This efficiency can benefit businesses and consumers alike, promoting economic growth and fostering innovation.

14.4 Monetary Policy and Financial Stability

CBDCs provide central banks with enhanced tools for implementing monetary policy. With a digital currency, central banks can have more direct control over the money supply, enabling the implementation of innovative policy measures such as programmable money, targeted stimulus, and real-time economic data analysis. CBDCs can also enhance financial stability by providing regulators with increased visibility and oversight of transactions, reducing the risk of illicit activities.

14.5 Data Privacy and Security Considerations

Data privacy and security are critical considerations when it comes to CBDCs. Striking a balance between privacy and regulatory compliance is essential to protecting individuals' financial data while preventing money laundering, fraud, and other illicit activities. Robust security measures, such as encryption, decentralized infrastructure, and identity verification protocols, must be implemented to safeguard the integrity and privacy of CBDC transactions.

14.6 Interoperability and Cross-Border Payments

CBDCs have the potential to revolutionize cross-border payments by enabling instantaneous and cost-effective transactions. The interoperability of different CBDCs can facilitate seamless international transactions, eliminating the need for multiple intermediaries, reducing transaction fees, and increasing transaction speed. CBDCs can simplify cross-border trade, enhance financial integration, and foster economic cooperation between countries.

14.7 Challenges and Adoption Considerations

The adoption of CBDCs presents challenges that need to be addressed. Technological infrastructure, cybersecurity, regulatory frameworks, user adoption, and cross-border coordination are among the key considerations. The design of CBDCs should carefully balance innovation with the preservation of financial stability, privacy, and the integrity of monetary systems. Pilots, experimentation, and collaboration among central banks and stakeholders can help address these challenges and guide the successful implementation of CBDCs.

14.8 Impact on Financial Institutions and the Economy

CBDCs have the potential to reshape the role of financial institutions and the broader economy. Commercial banks may need to adapt their business models to coexist with CBDCs, offering additional services beyond traditional deposit-taking and lending. CBDCs can foster innovation in financial services, promote competition, and provide opportunities for new business models to emerge. The impact on monetary policy, interest rates, and the broader economy will depend on the design and implementation of CBDCs.

14.9 The Future of Money: Opportunities and Considerations

The Central Bank's Digital Currencies represent a significant step toward the future of money. The digitization of national currencies through CBDCs can foster financial inclusion, enhance efficiency, improve monetary policy effectiveness, and streamline cross-border transactions. However, careful consideration must be given to privacy, security, regulatory frameworks, and the collaboration between central banks and stakeholders. The successful implementation of CBDCs requires continuous adaptation, innovation, and collaboration to unlock their full potential and shape the future of global finance.

In this chapter, we have explored the concept of Central Bank Digital Currencies, their potential benefits and challenges, and their implications for the future of money. The digitization of national currencies through CBDCs has the potential to transform financial systems, promote financial inclusion, and enhance economic growth. As central banks and governments continue to explore and experiment with CBDCs, the subsequent chapters will delve deeper into the evolving landscape of digital currencies, blockchain technology, and their impact on reshaping the global financial ecosystem.

Chapter 15: The Socioeconomic Impact of Crypto

Cryptocurrencies have emerged as a disruptive force in the global financial landscape, with significant implications for various socioeconomic aspects. In this chapter, we will explore the socioeconomic impact of crypto, examining its influence on financial systems, economic empowerment, wealth distribution, innovation, and social inclusion.

15.1 Financial Inclusion and Economic Empowerment

Cryptocurrencies have the potential to foster financial inclusion by providing access to financial services for individuals and communities that are underserved or excluded from traditional banking systems. Through crypto, individuals can participate in the global economy, access financial services, engage in economic activities, and transact globally. This financial inclusion can empower individuals, promote economic growth, and reduce socioeconomic inequalities.

15.2 Wealth Distribution and Decentralization

Cryptocurrencies challenge traditional centralized financial systems by promoting decentralization. Through the use of blockchain technology, cryptocurrencies enable peer-to-peer transactions and remove the need for intermediaries. This decentralized nature has the potential to reshape wealth distribution by reducing the concentration of wealth and increasing economic opportunities for a broader population. Crypto also allows for micropayments and fractional ownership, enabling broader access to assets and investment opportunities.

15.3 Innovation and Entrepreneurship

Cryptocurrencies have fostered a wave of innovation and entrepreneurship. Blockchain technology, the underlying technology behind cryptocurrencies, has applications beyond finance, including supply chain management, healthcare, voting systems, and more. The decentralized and transparent nature of crypto enables innovative business models, decentralized applications (dApps), and the emergence of new economic ecosystems. This environment encourages creativity, collaboration, and disruptive ideas.

15.4 Alternative Financing and Crowdfunding

Crypto has transformed the way businesses raise capital through alternative financing mechanisms such as Initial Coin Offerings (ICOs), Security Token Offerings (STOs), and decentralized crowdfunding platforms. These methods allow entrepreneurs and projects to access funding from a global pool of investors, removing geographical barriers and traditional intermediaries. This democratization of fundraising provides opportunities for startups, encourages innovation, and diversifies investment opportunities for individuals.

15.5 Remittances and Cross-Border Transactions

Cryptocurrencies offer a more efficient and cost-effective solution for cross-border transactions and remittances. Traditional remittance methods often involve high fees, long processing times, and limited accessibility. Crypto provides an alternative by enabling faster and cheaper peer-to-peer transactions across borders, reducing costs for remittance senders, and increasing the amount received by recipients. This has a direct positive impact on individuals and families reliant on remittances for their livelihood.

15.6 Social Impact and Philanthropy

Crypto has also facilitated social impact initiatives and philanthropy. Cryptocurrencies enable transparent and traceable transactions, making it easier to track and ensure donations reach their intended beneficiaries. Crypto-based projects and foundations have emerged to address various social and environmental challenges, leveraging blockchain technology to enhance transparency, accountability, and efficiency in charitable activities.

15.7 Regulatory Challenges and Consumer Protection

The socioeconomic impact of crypto is not without challenges. Regulatory frameworks are still evolving, and there are concerns regarding investor protection, consumer rights, fraud prevention, and market integrity. Striking a balance between fostering innovation and ensuring regulatory compliance is crucial to protecting individuals and maintaining the stability of financial systems. Clear regulations and robust consumer protection measures are necessary to mitigate risks and ensure responsible use of cryptocurrencies.

15.8. Education and Digital Literacy

To fully harness the socioeconomic potential of crypto, education and digital literacy play a vital role. Promoting awareness, understanding, and responsible usage of cryptocurrencies is essential for individuals, businesses, and governments. Educational initiatives should focus on teaching individuals about the fundamentals of crypto, blockchain technology, digital security, and the risks and opportunities associated with this emerging ecosystem.

15.9: The Future of Socioeconomic Impact

The socioeconomic impact of crypto continues to evolve and expand as the technology matures and adoption grows. As cryptocurrencies become more integrated into traditional financial systems, governments, regulators, and industry stakeholders need to adapt to unlock the full potential of crypto while addressing challenges and ensuring the benefits are shared by all. Continued collaboration, research, and innovation will shape the future socioeconomic impact of crypto, transforming economies and societies worldwide.

In this chapter, we have explored the multifaceted socioeconomic impact of cryptocurrencies. From promoting financial inclusion and economic empowerment to driving innovation, wealth distribution, and alternative financing, crypto has the potential to reshape socioeconomic landscapes. However, challenges related to regulation, consumer protection, and digital literacy must be addressed to ensure responsible and inclusive adoption of cryptocurrencies. As we move forward, the subsequent chapters will delve deeper into the evolving dynamics of crypto and blockchain technology and their impact on industries, governance, and global economic systems.

End Note

In this book, we embark on a comprehensive exploration of cryptocurrencies, blockchain technology, and their far-reaching impact on various aspects of our lives. From understanding the rise of cryptocurrency to delving into the evolution of traditional economics, the impact on financial markets, and the transformative potential of blockchain technology, we journeyed through the intricacies of this rapidly evolving ecosystem.

Throughout these chapters, we examined the challenges and opportunities presented by cryptocurrencies, the role of central bank digital currencies in shaping the future of money, and the socioeconomic implications of this digital revolution. We explored the potential for financial inclusion, wealth distribution, innovation, and social impact while also addressing concerns surrounding regulation, consumer protection, and sustainability.

As we conclude this book, it is evident that cryptocurrencies and blockchain technology have the power to reshape financial systems, promote economic empowerment, and drive societal change. However, realizing the full potential of this transformative technology requires collaborative efforts, continuous learning, and responsible adoption. Governments, regulators, industry participants, and individuals must work together to strike a balance between fostering innovation and mitigating risks, ensuring that the benefits of cryptocurrencies are shared by all.

The future of cryptocurrencies and blockchain technology holds immense possibilities. As the landscape continues to evolve, it is crucial to stay informed, adapt to emerging trends, and embrace the opportunities presented by this digital revolution. Whether you are an investor, entrepreneur, policymaker, or simply an enthusiast, the knowledge and insights gained from this book will serve as a foundation for understanding and navigating the exciting and dynamic world of cryptocurrencies.

We hope that this book has provided valuable insights, sparked curiosity, and encouraged further exploration into the fascinating realm of cryptocurrencies. As the journey continues, let us embrace the opportunities, address the challenges, and together shape a future where cryptocurrencies and blockchain technology contribute to a more inclusive, innovative, and sustainable global society.

Thank you for joining us on this exploration of cryptocurrencies, blockchain, and their transformative potential.